To *all* those who believed in this project;
Cannon Beach, there is *no* other place like you...

CANNON BEACH

The ART, CUISINE, HISTORY & ATMOSPHERE of OREGON'S FAVORITE COASTAL VILLAGE

ADAM CARLSEN & DONALD MASTERSON

oceanrider

INTRODUCTION

Terry Brooks—Author

My wife introduced me to Cannon Beach when I first moved to the Pacific Northwest in 1987. I had never been to the Oregon Coast. She was a Washington State native and had summered as a girl all up and down it. She took me there because she knew how it would affect me. I still remember what it made me feel. There was such a sense of space and solitude. The ocean swept away from the long stretches of beach to infinity. The coastal bluffs and plains marked the beginning of new possibilities. Haystack Rock was a writer's wish come true, a place of imagining and dreams.

I have written about Cannon Beach and its surroundings in several of my books since. I don't think there is a writer who has visited who could avoid doing so. I wrote about it as a real place and as a recreation of my imagination. But you would recognize it either way. The Oregon coast is unmistakable. The difficulty comes in trying to do it justice. Words aren't enough. Even pictures don't capture it adequately. The best you can do is to catch a glimpse here and a glimpse there. You have to be physically present, standing in one place so that you can turn around and around and see it all at once.

We go to Cannon Beach every year several times. We go to vacation, but we go to renew ourselves, as well. Walking the beach at sunset, poking through the various stores in the town, and driving down little roads we haven't visited before – it's all a way of finding ourselves, too. A writer needs to recharge the old writing batteries now and again; that's what Cannon Beach and the Oregon coast do for me.

It is worth mentioning that a trip to Cannon Beach anticipates weather of all sorts. What makes the Oregon coast so interesting is Mother Nature's unpredictability. She may prove sunny and warm. She may turn rainy and cold. She may offer storms with winds that threaten to rip the clothes from your back or calmness and sweet scents that remind you of childhood. You don't go to the coast for a particular experience; you go for whatever she chooses to give you.

SAND CASTLE DAY

JUNE 14, 1986 · CANNON BEACH, OR

TOLOVANA
VISITOR INFORMATION
ECOLA STATE PARK

OREGON

VISITORS
INFORMATION

LEWIS AND CLARK
TRAIL

TO HWY 101

COCKTAILS Good Food
Seafood

FORWARD

Adam Carlsen & Donald Masterson

What is Cannon Beach to you? By appearance, it's a small coastal town, population 1600, on the North Oregon Coast approximately 75 miles west of Portland, Oregon. For those who have walked the gallery-lined streets, jumped in the surf, or strolled down the beach to their favorite coffee shop in a sunrise silhouette, it might be just a bit more.

The answers are indeed as varied as the people who visit this unique and beautiful coastal spot. Perhaps Cannon Beach is a handful of salt-water taffy, a favorite meal of fresh seafood at an oft-visited restaurant, or a certain flaming sunset where for one breath, the sky exploded shades of purple and orange. Travel back to a hidden beach where loves first words were whispered. Recall the unexpected connection made with an artist's creation at one of many original galleries. Or perhaps the art was found in the architecture of that dream-like beach house you finally found. A magical shell discovered as a kid, a favorite surf break, a sand dollar housing angels, a giant rock, or a raging winter storm; Cannon Beach is many things to many people. Yet all those with such experiences would agree; there is something more to this town than just shops, galleries, hotels, restaurants, and beaches. These places serve as gracious hosts to the myriad of memories that make a piece of Cannon Beach your very own.

A certain magic resides here, with the power to shape unforgettable memories and capture hearts time and again. This is Cannon Beach, a place of experience and memory; where the simple recollection of time spent, has the ability to put a smile on your face.

In this book, we seek to reveal the heart and essence of Cannon Beach through the mediums of art, cuisine, history, and photography. Our desire is to capture moods and connotations, to evoke emotion, and touch feelings. Somewhere beneath the commercial bustle of Cannon Beach, there lies the magical reality of what draws us all to this special place by the sea. We hope you will recognize a bit of your own experience somewhere in these pages. If, through this work, forgotten memories are recaptured or an unexpected smile surfaces, then we have succeeded. Cannon Beach is more than a location that ends at a highway entrance, more than a place of weekend getaways and summer vacations; it is an ideal that lives in anyone who cares to make a memory here. *Enjoy...*

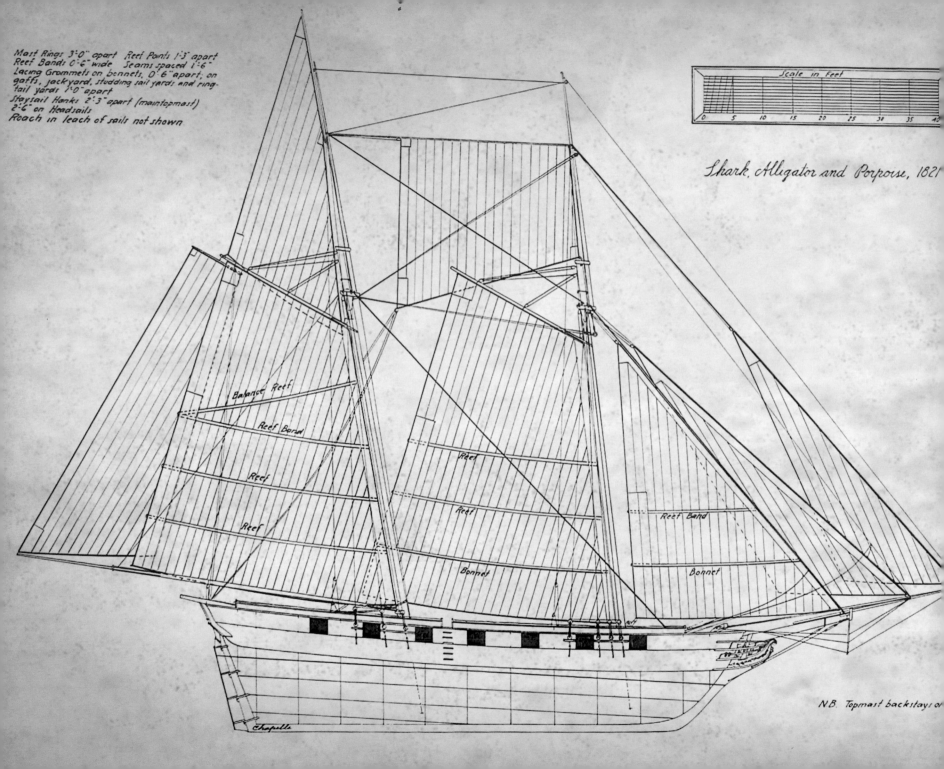

Mast Rings 3'-0" apart   Reef Points 1'-3" apart
Reef Bands 0'-6" wide   Seams spaced 1'-6"
Lacing Grommets on bonnets, 0'-6" apart; on
gaffs, jackyard, studding sail yards and ring-
tail yards 1'-0" apart
Staysail Hanks 2'-3" apart (maintopmast)
2'-6" on Headsails
Roach in leach of sails not shown

Scale in Feet

0   5   10   15   20   25   30   35   40

Shark, Alligator and Porpoise, 1821

Balance Reef

Reef Band

Reef

Reef

Reef

Reef

Reef Band

Bonnet

Bonnet

N.B. Topmast backstays of

Chapelle

Jackyard

Reef Band

Square Sail Boom

rs at waterways

History

CANNON BEACH IS A SMALL COASTAL VILLAGE
with a colorful history. A Lewis and Clark adventure, a logging community,
an errant cannon, a lighthouse known as "Terrible Tilly", and a visitor's
destination-all are a part of the Cannon Beach story.

The still evolving tale of this Oregon coastal jewel is steeped in
captivating visual and oral storytelling. From early pioneers to business
entrepreneurs—tidal waves to town marketing schemes, the historical
tapestry of Cannon Beach hangs above an ever-burning fireplace.
Moments, events, people have come and gone, and we remember through
story and image.

<"USS SCHOONER SHARK"
The original cannon washed ashore
after the ship sank giving Cannon Beach its name.
Picture courtesy of Smithsonian Institution, NMAH/Transportation

about 25 yds

Fork the Tribes △
of Calamox   by town

△

You Con Tribes
of Calamox big town

△   E-slitch or Fork
of Calamox

Center fr. from Naines Creek

Creek or Shinann
Creek

Natchees Tribes △ △
of Calamox   big town

Calamox
Nat. Ce Tribe

New Lot or white Crik

A House of Calamox
Nee Ne-cost Ty

Calamox River
85 yds deep tide

△   Whale

House of an old Town
Several Canoes with wood
Square Coppers in them

Point of Clarks View
Mountain about 300 feet high

A SHORT HISTORY of CANNON BEACH

No history of Cannon Beach is complete without mention of this area's original settlers and earliest pioneers. For thousands of years, the native Tillamook Indians occupied plots of coastal land ranging from Tillamook Head to as far south as the Siletz River near Tillamook. Several families often occupied cedar plank homes constructed at the mouths of coastal rivers and streams. It was not uncommon for two families to occupy one house. Subsistence from the earth and sea—salmon, whitefish, shellfish game, berries and herbs—were a regular part of the Tillamook diet.

Sadly, by the time the Lewis and Clark expedition arrived on the Oregon Coast in 1806, all native populations in the Lower Columbia River region had been reduced severely by disease. Introduced by early white explorers and fur traders, malaria, smallpox, syphilis, and measles spread with a vengeance, eventually reaching the Tillamook population further south.

‹CLARK'S MAP
Captain William Clark's first hand
drawn map of the Cannon Beach area.
(Top of map faces south)

Picture courtesy of Yale Collection of Western Americana, Beinecke Rare Book and Manuscript Library

LEWIS and CLARK

The Lewis and Clark Expedition's first interaction with the native Tillamook Indians occurred in January of 1806 in Cannon Beach. Having heard rumors from natives of a whale beached nearby, Captain William Clark set out with 12 men and Sacagawea to acquire much needed whale blubber and oil. Traveling south from their encampment, now known as Fort Clatsop, they spent the night on Tillamook Head. Awakening the next morning, the party began an early descent into Cannon Beach. It was here that Clark recorded in his diary the first known description of Cannon Beach, a timeless description of our beautiful area: "From this point I beheld the grandest and most pleasing prospect which my eyes ever surveyed." Continuing on, they forded a creek, named later by Clark "E Co-la" (Whale Creek), and came upon the 105-foot carcass of a whale. After acquiring 300 pounds of blubber and a few gallons of oil, they started the long trek back. This was to be the last we hear of the Cannon Beach area for decades.

THE FAMOUS CANNON

In 1846, a United States Navy schooner called Shark foundered and sank while attempting to cross the Columbia Bar near Astoria. Wreckage, including what was said to be three cannons, washed ashore near Hug Point just south of Cannon Beach. It is said that a party of Indians and an U.S. Midshipman removed one of the cannons to a nearby creek-bed for safekeeping and named the area Cannon Beach. Due to weather and time, the cannon was eventually lost from memory.

However, the cannon's journey of significance was not over. Many years later, a winter storm revealed it's hiding place below Hug Point. In those days, a single man (or woman) generally carried coastal mail from point to point on a horse. On one such route, mail carrier Bill Luce discovered the lost cannon. It was soon removed to sit in front of the Austin House, an early traveler's lodge, and eventually ended up in the hotel's barn.

In the years following, the cannon was moved to a place beside Highway 101, and in 1989 came to rest at the Astoria Heritage Museum—143 years after its journey had begun. Replicas have been made and displayed in various places as time has passed. They have been seen at both the North and South entrances into town and the local Historical Society.

EARLY CANNON BEACH AREA SETTLERS

In 1890, a roughshod railroad was built between Young's Bay in Astoria and the coastal town of Seaside. Before this time, travelers to the coast had to endure a boat ride down the Columbia River from Portland, followed by a miserable stagecoach ride to Seaside. Travel from the north to the coast was now much easier, and some were beginning to set their sights a little further south.

Around this time the poet Arthur Symons wrote:"I would wash the dust of the world in a soft green flood; Here, between sea and sea, in the fairy wood, I have found a wave-green solitude."

Truly, these words capture what early adventurers must have been feeling. Like today's travelers, they were seeking a place where they could leave the world behind, and find solitude in the music of the forests and sea. Few places offered more solitude than the Cannon Beach area, which was at that time called Elk Creek.

Very soon after the railroad was completed, a rough toll-road was built following an old Indian trail through the forest from Seaside. Rugged, untouched terrain and a single road leading in and out required early Elk Creek settlers to be a hardy bunch. Wood for housing and fires was plentiful and food was abundant. Deer, elk, bear, ducks and berries could be found in the forests, while fish and shellfish abounded in the Pacific Ocean. Travel to Seaside and beyond was by necessity only, perhaps to visit a doctor, or to acquire staples such as flour, sugar, salt, and oil. Traveling by car today, the trip would take approximately 10 minutes. Not so for these adventurers, as it was usually an all-day event!

Many of the early pioneers were bachelor males and among them were those known as "remittance men". By definition, remittance men were emigrants supported by remittances (financial allowances) from home. As legend has it, most were in exile from Europe and paid by their families to live as far away as possible.

Settlement and commerce were slow in coming to this part of the coast. South, near Hug Point, a Mr. James Austin built a traveler's stop called the Austin House. In 1891, it received distinction as a Post Office and was named Cannon Beach, after the still unfound cannon. The name Cannon Beach would not find its way north to the Elk Creek area until 1922.

In 1892, a sawmill proprietor by the name of Herbert Logan built the first hostelry within the boundaries of the Elk Creek area. The 16-room Logan House, later known as the Elk Creek Hotel, sat on the north side of Ecola Creek roughly where the Ecola Creek Lodge is located today. Herbert Logan and James Austin paved the way, and thus began the destination dreams of thousands yet to come...homesteaders, vacationers, honeymooners, dreamers and many more.

MAIN STREET- CANNON BEACH, OREGON.

POST OFFICE.
TOLOVANA PARK

Haystack Rock

THE EARLY RISE OF CANNON BEACH

Some years after the re-discovery of the lost cannon and following the original efforts of Herbert Logan and James Austin, concerted development in the Elk Creek area began to gain momentum. Understand that until 1910, Cannon Beach proper was only a collection of hardy settlers, courageous summer visitors, and the unofficial title "Elk Creek".

The nearest post office located at the Austin House south of Hug Point had been shut down in 1901. This meant that no post office existed anywhere between Seaside and Nehalem. In 1910, at the behest of Elk Creek's residents and summer visitors, a petition was made to Washington for a Post Office to be established in the community. It was soon approved. The area was given an official title, "Ecola", by the United States Government. Accordingly, the village of Elk Creek, now Ecola, was finally given formal recognition. It seems this event marked a transition for the community, as efforts to increase development in and around Ecola became more focused.

The years following 1910 saw a marked improvement in road quality in the area surrounding Ecola. Before this push, access from both the north and south had been difficult. A rough roadway was created at Hug Point; an area previously passable only during the lowest tides. The Seaside-Ecola road from the north was improved, reducing travel time to 30 minutes. And most importantly for Ecola, the creek at the north end was bridged, eliminating the previously unreliable ferry crossing.

With more solid roads came increasing access to this part of the coast, and a need for basic modern utilities such as water and telephone systems. In 1912 the first water system was built; primarily servicing 12 customers in the Mid-town area. Three years later a telephone system was installed, with 10 shared party lines. Ecola boasted fewer than 100 full-time residents at this time. Nonetheless, with these developments the community was slowly modernizing.

A logging camp and mill were established in approximately 1912, and more people began to settle in the area over the years following. This meant more children, and a subsequent need for a central school. The first classes were conducted in a local hotel, before being moved to a rented house. In 1921 a one-room schoolhouse was built specifically for educational purposes, but was often used for church services as well. Another major historic event was soon to occur, this time related less to structure, and more to the town's identity.

In 1912, the area south of Hug Point called Cannon Beach (where the cannon had originally appeared) was renamed Arch Cape. The name Cannon Beach was officially discarded. Soon after in 1922, the citizens of Ecola petitioned for a community name change. This attempt at change was primarily due to a growing number of postal mix-ups with a similarly named Willamette Valley town. The recently discarded name "Cannon Beach" was adopted by the community-never again to be changed.

TERRIBLE TILLY

The seas off the North Oregon Coast are thought to be some of the most treacherous in the world. Shipwrecks and tragedy were at one point such a normal occurrence that the area became known as "The Graveyard of the Pacific." Consequently, the need for a solid warning and lifesaving station became a necessity. It was commonly agreed upon that a lighthouse was the best solution.

Initially, it was thought that Tillamook Head between Seaside and Cannon Beach would provide the most practical location, but closer inspection would prove otherwise. Major G.L Gillespie, an army engineer, proposed the construction of a lighthouse atop Tillamook Rock off the north end of Cannon Beach. Research indicated that the most appropriate placement and operation of a lighthouse would need to be as close to sea level as possible. A lighthouse tender would then be employed to provide constant and vigilant service.

Construction of a lighthouse station atop Tillamook Rock would prove an emotionally and physically trying experience for all involved. The first attempt at mounting and measuring the rock occurred in 1879, when a revenue cutter from Astoria ordered by Major Gillespie approached the north side of the rock. The cutter was able to deposit two men on the rock; but threatening seas caused them to abandon their task and be rescued by lifelines.

A second, valiant effort provided the measurements necessary for construction; and in the fall of 1879 the lighthouse began to take form. Tragedy continued to plague the "Graveyard of the Pacific", only in a different form, as the first construction surveyor was swept off the rock to his death.

When "Terrible Tilly"; as the lighthouse would later become known, was finally completed in 1881, twenty-nine feet had been blasted off the top surface to allow for a sixty-nine foot tower containing a 48,000-candlepower lamp. Complementing the tower were two steam-operated "blasters" (foghorns), the lighthouse master's quarters, and the derrick which was used for supply loading and off-loading.

The years following would prove somewhat chaotic for Terrible Tilly, as monstrous seas would at times sweep over the rock; breaking lantern panes, threatening the roof, and flooding the building's interior. It became one of the most infamous lighthouses in the nation, thus coming to be known as "Terrible Tilly." 72 years after its original commission, the Tillamook Rock lighthouse-"Terrible Tilly"-was removed from service and replaced by an automated buoy. The comforting light for nearly a generation of Cannon Beach residents was silenced and the structure sits today as a ghostly remnant of a sometimes tragic, sometimes life-saving past.

Tillamook Lighthouse-Oregon Coast.

POST-1922 : A CHANGING IDENTITY

Many people and events in the years following the official naming of Cannon Beach all served, in their own way, to influence the development and identity of this town. Countless faces belong to this story, and all of the events that shaped our past are too numerous to capture in this abbreviated history. Needless to say, a few key events and people stand out, speaking to us through the corridor of history.

By 1922, Cannon Beach had finally received two significant progressions: formal recognition by the United States government, and a name that would endure. These events were a foreshadowing of both where Cannon Beach was headed, and of a changing identity. Looking back, the sequence of events appears very clear. The town continued to modernize, adopting new roads, plumbing, electricity, weekend homes and a more organized community structure. Hotels and traveler's stops became more and more frequent, and visitor traffic increased.

Before the 1920's and this new series of developments, activity in Cannon Beach was of the simple variety. Walks on the beach, frolicking in the sea, beach fires, and marshmallow roasts; locals and visitors were entertained by nature's bounty. Clamming, fishing, and crabbing were also common ways to find entertainment. In the twenties, this recreational focus would change, keyed by four ground breaking additions: the natatorium, the roller rink, the horseback-riding stables, and the moving-picture show. The natatorium-or "Nat" as it was called, was a swimming pool located on the north end of downtown, next to where the Cannon Beach Conference Center's Beach Front Lodge is today. Water was drawn on high tide through a pipe in Ecola Creek, heated first with cord wood and later burning oil. The "Nat" also featured a viewing balcony, which was, at the time, a favorite place to dance.

On the site of the present Coaster Theater, was the roller-rink. One local resident recalls how important the roller-rink was for Cannon Beach's younger residents. It was a place for boys to meet girls and show off their roller-skills. During one such visit, she also recalls taking a tumble and breaking out two of her front teeth in the process! All things considered, probably not the best way to impress a boy.

The first moving-picture shows were featured at both the natatorium and the roller-rink. It was not uncommon for attendees to bring their own seats, and the show itself was sometimes projected on an outside wall. The fourth significant addition to Cannon Beach recreation was the horseback riding stables, one located along Ecola Creek and the other south near Haystack Rock. "Growing up," recalls one local resident, "all us kids in town led horse tours at one time or another. It was our primary summer occupation."

Cannon Beach was truly changing and the events mentioned marked a major transition for the town. More recreational activities existed, and visitors were becoming much more common, with some staying for entire summers. The town began to experience growth on a level previously unfelt. The future for Cannon Beach looked bright indeed.

Street Scene - Cannon Beach - Ore - 5-61 Smith

THE DECADES FOLLOWING WORLD WAR II

The decades following World War II in Cannon Beach were characterized by an overriding theme of growth and expansion. Different photographs of the downtown corridor, separated by year and decade, are stunning in their variety. The cars, people, and buildings captured on film over the years, present an ever-changing face of Cannon Beach.

One of the most important events marking the immediate post-war growth era was the establishment of the Cannon Beach Conference Center. It first began in 1944, when a Portland minister by the name of Archibald McNeil and his wife, Evangeline, acquired the Cannon Beach Hotel on the northern end of downtown. Mr. and Mrs. McNeil's intent was to establish a non-denominational family church camp unlike most in Oregon at the time. Another goal was to provide recreation and rest to accompany various religious programs. Over the years, the Cannon Beach Conference Center has grown exponentially from its original, humble beginnings. In many ways, the center has been a crucial component in the historical tapestry of Cannon Beach, and in 1995 celebrated its 50th anniversary.

It was right around this time that the town at large took care of some much-needed structural business. Cannon Beach installed asphalt sidewalks to replace what were a series of unreliable wooden boardwalks. A commercial club (Boosters) was formed to provide for the town's basic needs, and a fire department was created after a house burned to the ground. New businesses, buildings, and streets were springing up everywhere. The population increased and utility improvements continued to occur. In 1950, a new highway was completed, reducing travel time from Portland to an hour and a half, and eliminating a daunting descent into town: the 111 curves that had held many visitors at bay for years.

One adage had remained constant since Cannon Beach's earliest days: An increase in accessibility equaled an increase in visitor traffic and tourism. It seemed that incorporation was a necessary step; but to some this implied unwanted growth. After much local debate and controversy, Cannon Beach was finally officially incorporated in 1955. This particular year marked another transition, and some might say, a starting point. Over the next four decades, the town would continue to grow, fueled by the natural beauty of the surrounding environment, and the clever promotion of a handful of groups and individuals. The first major event was the Sandcastle competition, which became known worldwide and continues to this day.

According to one prominent local resident, the current state and character of Cannon Beach would not have been possible without the efforts of two early visionaries, Maurie Clark and Ray Watkins. In the early 1960's, the town was showing signs of age and dilapidation. Fueled by Watkins aesthetic creativity and Clark's philanthropy, a variety of building projects were undertaken and finished. Examples include the Coaster Theater, Mariner Market, the library, and the Chamber of Commerce building. The result of their work was an overall enhancement and beautification of Cannon Beach, and this attitude proved to be contagious. Residential districts were improved, and a physical transformation was completed over time.

This transformation would spur other changes in character and identity. Cannon Beach would become an art community; not really a surprise, considering the beauty of the natural surroundings. Tourism would continue to flourish, soon becoming the primary commercial industry. Cannon Beach was becoming what it is today; an economy built on tourism and travel, a place to retire, and the most unique and beautiful town on the Oregon Coast.

"Cannon Beach Oregon"

Cannon Beach, Oregon

JEFFREY Hull

Art & Atmosphere

OUR VILLAGE SEQUESTERED BETWEEN NORTH coast headlands has retained its pull and draw on the public imagination for decades. Few places in the world possess such remarkable features of natural beauty in mutual concordance. Consider its setting. I like the term "setting" because it reminds me of jewelry. I think of our small coastal community as a precious jewel "set", as a jeweler would phrase the placement of a rare stone, between treed promontories north and south, the coast range mountains east, and the westerly pacific. We existed slightly off the well-worn track for most of our history here, a special destination unknown to many. That, of course, has changed.

I live here for many reasons: a surfeit of natural prospects bounded by our splendid sea, a tempered climate, creatures and vegetation in profusion, a hint of isolation from proximal urban hubs, sweeping daily climatological change, sweet pelagic air, and seasons one can count on year after year. Our township has a history of generating a minestrone-rich broth of characters, diverse and interesting. I savor this rich vein of quirkiness. Those of us who live and visit here are truly favored.

Peter Lindsey
Author of "Comin' in Over the Rock: A Storyteller's History of Cannon Beach"

HAYSTACK ROCK : OUR FAVORITE MONOLITH

Coastal Highway 101 was originally constructed to pass directly through Cannon Beach. Visitor traffic hugging the pacific coastline had no choice but to pass through the town center, and in turn directly through the local business district. Cannon Beach businesses had no complaints; they were visible to travelers, and little outside promotion was necessary. All this changed when plans were made to redirect the path of Highway 101 to its present location outside the downtown area. The highway was moved, and many folks began to worry about how such an event would affect visitor traffic and the overall visibility of Cannon Beach.

Accounts and versions of the following tale vary. According to some locals, the highway's move prompted a very interesting response. Certain local business owners took matters into their own hands by concocting a zany promotional scheme that makes current town marketing efforts appear downright lifeless in comparison. Somehow in the course of their planning, they neglected to consider certain aspects of the surrounding natural environment. Haystack Rock has long been Cannon Beach's signature. This monolithic granite structure towers 235 feet above the sand and is one of the largest "sea-stacks" on the Pacific coast. In fact, the rock is considered to be the third largest free-standing monolith in the world.

Upon descending into Cannon Beach, Haystack Rock captures the eye immediately. The local business schemers decided to place their bets on Haystack Rock's draw, and positioned spotlights directly on the rock to be seen from the recently distanced Highway 101. In theory, travelers passing by would be captured by the over-lit presence of the rock and compelled to make Cannon Beach a stopping point.

Hilariously and tragically, they failed to account for the multitude of birdlife residing on the rock's face. Bright lights and constant glare disrupted the sea-birds' natural pattern of life. Unable to sleep or function normally, they quickly became disoriented. Over the following week, reminiscent of Alfred Hitckcock's "The Birds", the poor creatures lashed out in confusion and fear. Driven from their home, the seabirds flew over town and left their mark on cars, houses, and anything else in their path, including unsuspecting beach wanderers! The use of spotlights to illuminate Haystack Rock was immediately discontinued, and the grateful seabird community settled back to life as normal.

THE CHANGING FACE OF TOURISM

Cannon Beach has undoubtedly become one of the West Coast's most desirable tourist destinations. Our visitor contingent is as inseparable from the town's identity as our local population. The face of tourism in Cannon Beach is ever-changing. In the early days, most were visiting loggers here in the area to make a tough living. Today, most are vacationers, looking to escape to the beach for a brief respite.

The passage of years in Cannon Beach has been accompanied by a developing identity, both on a micro and macro scale. Consequently, we are left with a unique village atmosphere, where visitors and tourism affect town character as much as local people and small-town life. Modern Cannon Beach is a single, cohesive unit, with two distinct heads: tourism and local village life. Although elements of both are very different, they co-exist within the fabric of life in this coastal community.

The local/tourist relationship has characterized Cannon Beach for the past 50 years, but the trappings have changed significantly as time has passed. Today, visitors will often rent a hotel room or beach cabin for one day to one week depending upon their unique vacation schedule. It was not always this way. In the 1950's –1960's, visiting families would usually spend an entire summer from Memorial Day to Labor Day. They would move into a family beach house and call Cannon Beach home for the next three to four months. Most were from the Portland area. Local children recall making friends that would return at the same time each year. As you might guess, the line dividing local from tourist during this time was thin indeed.

The intimate nature of the local/tourist relationship would change with time and the evolving accessibility of Cannon Beach as a travel destination. Technology would continue to develop, thus shortening distance and travel time. Better coastal roads were constructed and travelers found it easier to get away for shorter periods without compromising work and schedules. The days of Cannon Beach as a long-term holiday destination began to fade, and a new model would soon evolve.

EVERY TIME WE WALK

ALONG A BEACH SOME ANCIENT
URGE DISTURBS US SO THAT
we find ouselves shedding shoes *and*
garments *or* scavenging among seaweed
and whitened timbers like *the* homesick
refugees *of* a long war. *Loren Eiseley*

THE TIDAL WAVE SCARE OF '64

In 1964 the first and only Tidal Wave (Tsunami) in recent memory shattered the relative safety of Cannon Beach. Spawned by an earthquake off the coast of Alaska, the wave had dissipated significantly by the time it reached the Oregon Coast. However, residents were asked to evacuate, as the exact magnitude of the approaching wall of water was largely unknown.

One resident recalls climbing on top of an old gym owned by the Cannon Beach Conference Center to observe the wave's progress. Probably not the most prudent approach, but such an event had never been witnessed in the modern memory of Cannon Beach.

The wave struck, rushing up local Ecola Creek, destroying the bridge, and spilling onto the city streets. Ecola Creek Lodge, then known as the Bell Harbor Motel, sustained damage as did the local elementary school. Attendees of Cannon Beach Elementary School remember that until the early 2000's, swing-set poles at the school remained twisted and scarred; a lingering snapshot of what had occurred.

Due to the tidal wave scare of 1964, Cannon Beach is naturally very sensitive to the ever-changing moods of its neighbor, the Pacific Ocean. Over the years following, residents have at times been forced to higher ground when the possibility of a tsunami has threatened. As a visitor on a weekday evening, you may be startled by the thundering sound of cows mooing, followed by a robotic warning voice. Don't be alarmed, it's simply Cannon Beach's state of the art "COWS" (community tsunami warning system) being tested.

Today you will find that Cannon Beach is well prepared should another wave strike. Informational signs can be found around town, and the police force and local rescue workers are well trained on the off chance that another major tidal event occurs. As a coastal community you can never be too prepared!

There are *no* waves *without WIND.*
Ancient Chinese Proverb

ROLL ON, THOU DEEP AND DARK BLUE

OCEAN—ROLL! TEN THOUSAND FLEETS SWEEP OVER
thee in vain; Man marks the earth with ruin—his control
stops with the shore. *Lord Byron "Childe Harold's Pilgrimage" 1818*

THE CANNON BEACH SURF EXPERIENCE

It may come as a surprise that the cold, often forbidding seas off the coast of Cannon Beach contain a variety of well-respected surfing spots. During the summer when temperatures rise and the mighty Pacific Ocean mellows, surfers from all over the Northwest and beyond flock to their favorite surf spots known as "Breaks". On a soft summer day, surfers can be seen bobbing beyond the breaking waves and waiting for the swell of an approaching wave set. Don't let your eyes and the black hooded suits fool you, those are in fact surfers and not sea lions! Frigid waters force surfers to wear full body neoprene wetsuits, gloves and boots (booties) to stay warm. While water temperatures rise a bit during the summer and fall, they still average in the low 50's year round.

Cannon Beach area surf breaks even have special names and slang references, coined by the surfer population over the years. The most famous break, located at Oswald West State Park, is known as "Short Sands", or "Shorties". Two parking lots with access to this beach sit directly off Highway 101, seven miles south of Cannon Beach. An approximate one-half mile walk through thick forest and foliage reveals the beautiful cove beach known as "Short Sands". On any given summer day, the water is filled with surfers of all ages and skill levels. Locals say that this is definitely the best place for a beginner.

Another well-known break is at Indian Beach, located just north of world-renowned Ecola State Park. Surfers park in a lot overlooking the beach before taking a short trail down. Much like Short Sands, Indian Beach's waves break in what is commonly called a cove. Surfers favor the cove setting due to the relative shelter offered against the full force of the Pacific Ocean. Waves traveling into a cove will not hit with the same force as they would on an open beach. The outcropping north and south rock wall will cause a swelling wave to wrap in, tempering the fury, and create favorably breaking waves that are perfect for riding.

The commercial popularity of surfing in Cannon Beach, and on the west coast in general, has grown exponentially in recent years. Local surfers claim to have felt the influx of interest in this formerly alternative sport. Surf package rentals, usually including a surfboard, wetsuit, neoprene boots, and gloves, fly out of local surf shops during the summer. Hollywood films, trendy sitcoms, and "surfer" clothing lines have contributed to the growing popularity of surfing and have added a certain aura of "cool". For many, this image is very attractive, and Cannon Beach provides an outlet for a growing trend.

THERE IS pleasure in the pathless woods, THERE IS rapture in the lonely shore, THERE IS society where none intrudes, by the deep sea, and music in its roar; I love not man less, but nature more. *George Gordon Byron*

MY LIFE IS LIKE A STROLL UPON
THE BEACH, AS NEAR THE OCEAN'S EDGE
as I can go. *Henry David Thoreau*

SOFT EVENINGS AND BEACH FIRES

Most would agree that a beach fire with friends and family on a soft summer evening is one of life's great pleasures. Roasting marshmallows, making s'mores, watching the stars, and enjoying the peaceful pace of beach life make this event timeless.

Stroll the shores on a calm summer night and you can enjoy a panoramic north and south view, with dozens of flickering orange dots highlighted against the inky blackness. It's not uncommon during this time of year to see 30+ sparkling beach fires stretching the length of Cannon Beach until late into the evening. If you don't have wood or fire starting materials, don't worry. Simply walk the beach and you will probably come upon a few vacant fires left burning like silent beacons.

The beach bonfire experience also has a darker side. Most folks don't realize how dangerous it is to bury a beach fire with sand to smother the flames. Doing so will sometimes create an oven-like area beneath the sand, where smoking embers and heat become trapped to create blistering sub-surface temperatures. To make matters worse, these sand ovens are rarely visible from the surface. Most days, walking barefoot on the beach is a simple pleasure, but be cautious and watch your step! Over the years, both adults and children have encountered these natural ovens firsthand (or feet). As you can imagine, the results were less than pleasurable.

I EXPERIENCE A PERIOD OF FRIGHTENING CLARITY IN THOSE MOMENTS WHEN NATURE IS so beautiful. I am no longer sure of myself, and the paintings appear as in a dream. *Vincent Van Gogh*

OREGON'S GREATEST TREASURE

Over the last few years, Cannon Beach has received both national and worldwide recognition as a top beach destination. Most visitors and locals would claim not to be surprised by these accolades. When considering the multitude of American and worldwide beach destinations, this is quite an achievement. Honors include:

- ✦ The Travel Channel—America's #1 beach for romance

- ✦ The Travel Channel—World's top 10 best beach destination 2002 and 2004

- ✦ The Travel Channel—America's #7 best North American sandcastle contest

- ✦ Travel Channel Feature in 2004. Local businesses highlighted included:
Once Upon A Breeze Kite Shop, Mike's Bike Shop and The Surfsand Resort.

- ✦ Conde Naste—Top West Coast Beaches 2002

- ✦ USA Today Newspaper—Top 12 North American Beaches

- ✦ National Geographic Magazine—Top 12 Beaches 2003

- ✦ National Geographic TV Channel's Best Unknown Beaches in North America 2003-04

Undoubtedly, Cannon Beach will continue to receive recognition, as the magic and romance of Oregon's favorite coastal village continues to be discovered.

HOLLYWOOD COMES TO CANNON BEACH

Small-town Cannon Beach has played host to Hollywood at times over the years. You may remember a hit movie called "The Goonies", produced in 1984. Cannon Beach residents recall the sight of cars racing on the beach just north of Haystack Rock, with cameras and a production crew following close behind. It seemed a very unusual event at the time, but turned out to be a scene filmed for "The Goonies" on our beautiful shores. Film crews later moved up to Ecola State Park and the road leading in, to complete crucial scenes for the movie.

A few years later in 1990, Arnold Schwarzenegger and film crews came to town. Once again, they chose Ecola State Park to film a scene for the movie "Kindergarten Cop." Mr. Schwarzenegger, governor of California and action star, was seen biking through the streets of Cannon Beach, eating at local restaurants, and filming at our famous park. Star-struck local children followed him around town and lingered around the movie set, hoping to score a brief apperance as an extra. For a small coastal town, it was quite a memorable event.

In 1991, the final scene for the movie "Point Break" was filmed at Indian Beach just north of Ecola State Park. Some Cannon Beach locals were cast as extras in the final scene, visible as the primary characters make their way down to the beach. Viewers may also recall the film's climax, where two characters struggle and fight in the surf. Images of the mammoth breaking waves were actually filmed in Australia, but the beach is our own.

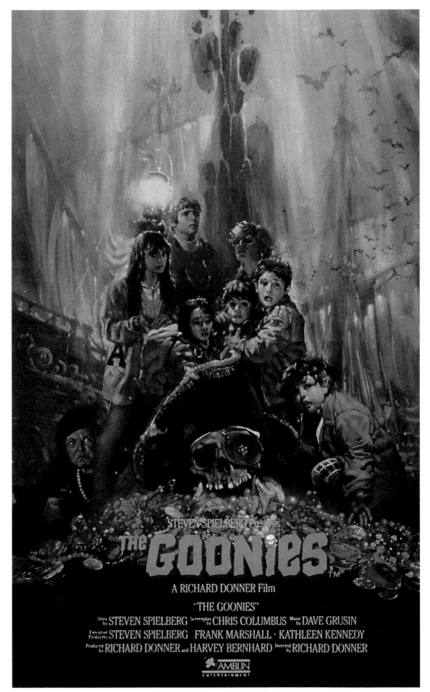

STEVEN SPIELBERG Presents

THE GOONIES

A RICHARD DONNER Film
"THE GOONIES"
Story by STEVEN SPIELBERG Screenplay by CHRIS COLUMBUS Music by DAVE GRUSIN
Executive Producers STEVEN SPIELBERG FRANK MARSHALL · KATHLEEN KENNEDY
Produced by RICHARD DONNER and HARVEY BERNHARD Directed by RICHARD DONNER

AMBLIN
ENTERTAINMENT

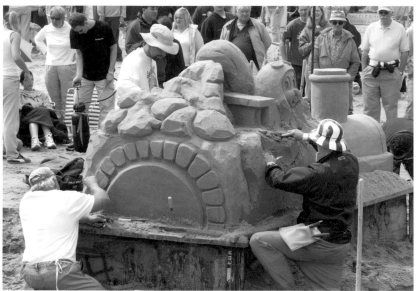

SANDCASTLE CONTEST

The first sandcastle contest weekend in Cannon Beach was said to be established in defiant response to the Tsunami of 1964. Local residents began holding an annual beach based celebration on the day of the lowest tide of the year. Attendees were invited to build a sandcastle, or any other sand construction that tickled their fancy. The original entrance fee was a quarter, and participants received a bag of saltwater taffy.

In an attempt to commercialize this event, Cannon Beach later moved the day to fall on the lowest weekend tide of the year. This allowed visitors to more readily attend, and the event soon grew to mammoth proportions. Sandcastle Day in Cannon Beach became the town's first major tourist attraction and a smashing success known around the country. Each year both professionals and amateurs enter the contest, and the final results are often spectacular. Many of these sand constructions are true works of art that take hours to complete. Over the years, sandcastle weekend visitor populations have at times approached 30,000, with a current average of approximately 10,000 per year. What a staggering numeric increase from the 1,600 full-time residents who call Cannon Beach home.

ANNUAL SANDCASTLE DAY

1996 1997 1998 1999 2000

2001 2002 2003 2004 2005

SANDCASTLE DAY 1996

cannon beach

Sand Castle

35th SANDCASTLE '98

CANNON BEACH
OREGON JUNE

SPONSORS

Sandcastle
Festival
June 5, 1999

sand castle

long ago in a century gone by, here in this place
where great mountains cool their craggy toes in
the mightiest of seas, great castles once stood.
Only the small village of Cannon Beach remains,
all else taken by the sea. They have returned
these castles of sand, these ramparts of dreams,
they have returned, being built by men, women,
and children, in this year 2000,
...and i am their witness...

n Beach, Oregon
ndcastle Day
une 1, 2002

SANDCASTLE DAY
JUNE 14, 2003
Cannon Beach, Oregon

40th ANNUAL
SANDCASTLE CONTEST
JUNE 5, 2004
Cannon Beach, Oregon

June 11, 2005

POSTERS of THE

1976   1977   1978   1979   1980

1981   1982   1983   1984   1985

CANNON BEACH
as IT WAS in 1965

THE CANNON

GAZETTE

A COMMUNITY NEWSPAPER
TO BRING
UNDERSTANDING
THROUGH COMMUNICATION

Serving
Cannon Beach
Tolovana Park
Arch Cape

VOL. 1 NUMBER 7   THURSDAY SEPTEMBER 2, 1976   PRICE 10 CENTS

Scenes from

Summer '76

Summer of '76 is about to fade away behind Haystack Rock for another year, but not without leaving behind memories of of some fun, and some important events.

The Cannon GAZETTE "hits the streets" June 3, 1976.

July 4th Frolicks!

A surprised visitor strolls into an historic moment at library.

The biggest Sandcastle Day ever.

"Dragon" steals show in parade

SUMMER

How cool the air flows from the west
at the turn of the summer evening,
off the fog that lies along the coast
over the mountains, and soft, and long.

Softness of the evening air,
softness of water on the tongue;
longer than mountains these endure,
longer maybe than anything.

DECEMBER

Snow on the wind among the rain,
a dark east wind.
A crow flies the hard way.
Winter is my mind.

Gusts of smoke, ghosts of snow
through the old trees
blow on the crow's wind
to a cold sea.

CANNON BEACH POEMS

©URSULA K. LE GUIN

SPRING SPARROW SONG

Hear me so sweetly

start to repeat it,

pause and complete it.

AUTUMN

A calm evening of October.

I am reluctant to lose a light so golden.

Flung upward from the western water

it turns the under-branches

of the dying spruce to a dark glory.

I will wear into winter

this thin gold armor.

THE SEASONS OF CANNON BEACH

Cannon Beach is driven by seasons, though not necessarily defined by the distinct weather patterns common to other areas of the country. People, events and atmosphere mark the changing seasons with a sense of waxing/waning activity, and each has a unique sentiment.

Winter in Cannon Beach can only be called spectacular. Mighty storms sweep off the Pacific Ocean, attacking the landscape with the force of an invading army. Breaking waves slam into sea and rock walls, foaming like a shaken soda pop. Trees sway under winds reaching 100+ miles-per-hour, and human life hibernates in warmth and safety. Its not unusual for the sky to break, revealing cool, sunny skies. The Christmas season is highlighted by a series of community events; most notably the traditional lamp-lighting ceremony.

Spring holds a sense of expectance, not unlike waiting for weekend visitors. Mid-March brings the first significant swell of visitors after the long winter; spring-breakers on respite from daily work and school. The artist community releases the fruits of their winter-long toil during "Spring Unveiling". Galleries and artists display their work throughout town, and folks are able to browse at their leisure. Late May brings Memorial Day Weekend, a holiday that signifies the real transition from spring to summer.

Summer in Cannon Beach is the focal point of the year's progressing sense of activity. Sandcastle Day is the first major event to usher in the new season. Fourth of July weekend kicks-off the true visitor's season and the town teems with life until Labor Day. The weather is warm and clear, and people come and go daily.

Fall is the most delicately beautiful season of the year on the coast. The air is soft and warm, and life slows its pace. The Stormy Weather Arts Festival highlights the town's thriving artistic community. This has become a very popular event in Cannon Beach, as people travel from all over to walk-through galleries, meet their favorite artists, listen to live music, and participate in a series of planned events. Local artists convene on a weekend night, to show off their skills in a "quick-draw" event. They create a piece in one hour, and spectators bid on each auction style. This event is the highlight, and conclusion of a wonderful season!

Cuisine

CANNON BEACH HOSTS A VARIETY OF DINING destinations, many of which are steeped in coastal tradition and flavor. The following pages highlight recipes and imagery drawn from our fine local restaurants. Enjoy a wide range of selections, from the western omelet to an intricately prepared New York striploin steak. You can now enjoy your favorite dish from that special restaurant, in the comfort of your own kitchen.

THE BISTRO

OWNED and OPERATED SINCE 1986, MATT and ANITA DUEBER and THE BISTRO STAFF HAVE SUCCEEDED IN MAINTAINING A CONSISTENT COMMITMENT TO ENJOYING A MEMORABLE MEAL.

TUCKED AWAY BEHIND a charming bricked courtyard and adjacent to Laurel's Wine Shop, you will find The Bistro. Owned and operated since 1986, Matt and Anita Dueber and The Bistro staff have succeeded in maintaining a consistent commitment to enjoying a memorable meal.

From the west end, a bay window allows a peak at the cozy atmosphere inside. With a full service lounge, candlelit dining, and local guitarist, Wes Wahrmund, on the weekends, the Bistro has become a destination restaurant when visiting Cannon Beach. They are open for dinner at 5:00 p.m. with the lounge opening at 4:30 p.m.

SESAME CRUSTED SALMON
with APRICOT VINAIGRETTE

Serves 4

INGREDIENTS

4 five oz. salmon fillets, skin off and pin bones removed

1 tbsp. sesame seeds

1 tsp. black pepper

1 tsp. coriander

1/4 tsp. salt

2 tbsp. olive oil, divided

1 cup apricot nectar

1/2 cup dried apricots, diced

1/2 cup red bell peppers, diced

1/4 cup rice wine vinegar

1 tbsp. minced ginger

1 tbsp. cornstarch

2 tbsp. cold water

METHOD

Pre-heat oven to 450°. Combine sesame seeds, pepper, coriander, and salt. Season salmon with this mixture. Heat 1 tbsp. olive oil over high heat in a 12 inch saute pan to hot, medium heat to soften, then add ginger, nectar, and vinegar, bringing to a boil.

In a small bowl, blend cornstarch with water, and pour into sauce, stirring well. Allow to simmer for 1 minute, then taste and season if necessary. Pour over salmon fillets.

Serves 8

INGREDIENTS

8 inch springform pan

Parchment paper

Aluminum foil

12 inch x 18 inch baking pan

1 tbsp. melted butter

8 tbsp. unsalted butter

10 oz. Callebaut Bittersweet Chocolate, chopped fine

7 eggs, separated

3/4 cup + 2 tbsp. granulated sugar

1/4 cup Meyer's Rum

METHOD

Place parchment paper over the bottom of an 8 inch springform pan, and secure by attaching to the side. Coat bottom and sides of pan with melted butter. Trim excess paper from around the pan. Place pan over aluminum foil and fold up side of pan at least 2 inches, sealing tightly.

Pre-heat oven to 400°. Add chocolate and butter into a stainless steel bowl and place over barely simmering water to melt.

Meanwhile, separate eggs into mixing bowls. Add 3/4 cup sugar to the yolks and beat on high speed until pale in color, 2–3 minutes. Beat egg whites on low speed until frothy. Increase speed to high and beat to very soft peaks. Reduce speed to medium and sprinkle in remaining 2 tbsp. sugar. Return to high speed and beat for 30 seconds.

Add egg yolks, rum, and 1/3 of egg whites to chocolate mixture. Whisk well to blend. With a spatula, fold in remaining egg whites gently, and pour into prepared pan. Place baking sheet into pre-heated oven and add hot water to cover bottom of pan. Place in center and bake for the following: 400° for 17 minutes, 350° for 17 minutes, 250 ° for 26 minutes.

Remove cake to a cooling rack. Cool slightly before serving with raspberry sauce and whipped cream.

CRAB CAKES *with* LEMON SAKE BUTTER

Serves 3

INGREDIENTS

Crab Cakes:

2 tbsp. green onion, minced

1 tsp. ginger, minced fine

4 cloves roasted garlic

1 cup Shitake Mushrooms, sliced

2 tsp. peanut oil

3/4 cup panko

1/4 cup flour

2 tsp. sesame oil

1 tbsp. lemon juice

1 whole egg

1/2 tsp. salt

1/2 tsp. fresh ground black pepper

3/4 cup milk

10 oz. fresh Dungeness Crab meat picked over for shells, and drained well

Mescaline salad greens

Lemon Sake Butter:

1/4 cup sake

1 tbsp. lemon juice

1 tbsp. cold butter

METHOD

Begin by heating peanut oil in an 8 inch sauté pan. Add Shitake Mushrooms and cook to soften. Cool. In medium sized bowl add all crab cake ingredients, and mix well. Cover and refrigerate for at least 30 minutes.

For 1 serving (crab cake), heat peanut oil in a 10 inch sauté pan until it is hot, but not smoking. With a 1/4 cup measuring apparatus, add 2 servings to the pan and flatten slightly, cooking over medium heat 2–3 minutes on each side to a golden brown.

Remove cakes to prepared platter, and wipe pan clean. Add sake with lemon juice and bring to a boil. Whisk in butter to thicken, and serve over crab cakes.

BELLA ESPRESSO

A TRIP TO BELLA ESPRESSO IS MUCH MORE THAN JUST A JAVA STOP, IT'S A DESTINATION EXPERIENCE DEFINED BY BEAUTY, ART, AND A FANTASTIC CUP OF COFFEE.

BELLA ESPRESSO WAS founded in 2001 by neighboring Pizza a' Fetta owner James Faurentino and local artist Donald Masterson. Their overriding goal was to create the feel of a genuine Italian coffee house influenced by James Faurentino's old world family history. Authenticity is important to the owners, and with this in mind, they decided early to import genuine gelato ice cream from the streets of Milan, Italy.

Along with their famous gelato, Bella Espresso features gourmet desserts, fresh fruit smoothies, a variety of coffee drinks, and their own brand of coffee roasting; Bella Roasta. You will be met by a warm and friendly staff, who's desire is to make your experience memorable. Perhaps most stunning is the wall and portrait art work created by Donald Masterson.

A trip to Bella Espresso is much more than just a java stop, it's a destination experience defined by beauty, art, and a fantastic cup of coffee.

BELLA SUNRISE SMOOTHIE

Serves 2

INGREDIENTS

1 1/4 cup passion fruit juice

1/4 cup half & half

5 scoops powdered white chocolate

3 fresh strawberries

1/2 cup diced mango

1/2 cup sliced peaches

1 scoop frozen vanilla yogurt

METHOD

Combine all ingredients into blender. Blend on high for 45 seconds. Serve in two 12 oz. glasses. Garnish with whip cream and mint leaf.

FRENCH KISS LATTE

Serves 1

INGREDIENTS

3 oz. espresso

11 oz. milk

2 scoops powdered white chocolate

1 oz. real DaVinci Caramel Sauce

1 oz. DaVinci Irish Cream

METHOD

Pour 2 shots of Bella Roasta espresso blend over all ingredients in a 16 oz. mug. Steam milk to desired temperature and stir into mug. Drizzle caramel sauce on top to garnish.

CLARK'S

WITH THE TABLE SPACE AND CAPABILITY TO HOST LARGER PARTIES, CLARK'S IS A WONDERFUL DESTINATION FOR FAMILIES. THERE IS SOMETHING FOR EVERY MANNER OF TASTE OR PREFERENCE.

CLARK'S RESTAURANT and Bar opened in 2001 on the site of the old Cannon Beach Lumberyard. The beautiful and spacious interior boasts stained hardwood floors and walls. Above, the ceiling rises expansively, criss-crossed by solid oak beams. Wall décor is classy, yet very hip and appropriate. A classically restored bicycle hangs suspended next to the fireplace and a collection of different domestic and micro-brew beer plaques adorn the walls. Most noticeable at Clark's is the warm-lit ambiance and distinct pub-feel of the main floor.

Warm yourself on a blustery day by the mammoth stone-built wood burning fireplace, or wet your palate at Clark's full service central bar. With the table space and capability to host larger parties, Clark's is a wonderful destination for families. There is something for every manner of taste or preference. Highly recommended for lunch, dinner, or a drink after hours.

SHRIMP SALAD SANDWICH
with CHIPOTLE MAYONNAISE

INGREDIENTS

Chipotle Mayonnaise:

2 chipotle peppers in Adobo sauce, diced fine

2 green onions, diced fine

1 cup loose cilantro leaves, diced fine

2 cups regular mayonnaise

Salt

Fresh ground pepper

4–5 drops Chalula pepper sauce

Shrimp Salad:

1 tbsp. chipotle mayonnaise

4–5 oz. Oregon Bay Shrimp

Rustic Italian or other good quality bread

Regular mayonnaise

1 strip crisp bacon, diced

1/2 fresh avocado

1 fresh tomato, sliced

1 leaf fresh lettuce

METHOD

Mix 4–5 oz. fresh Oregon bay shrimp with 1 heaping tbsp. of chipotle Mayonnaise. Spread regular mayonnaise on 2 slices of rustic Italian or other quality bread. Top 1 bread slice with a healthy spread of the shrimp mixture. Sprinkle diced, crisp bacon on top of shrimp mixture followed by diced avocado. Next place sliced tomato and crisp lettuce on top of mixture. Place other slice of bread over all to create sandwich, and cut in half before serving.

WOOD FIRED CEDAR PLANKED SALMON

Serves 1

INGREDIENTS

1 untreated cedar shingle, at least
4 inch x 12 inch. Soak in water.

8 oz. salmon fillet
(Wild salmon preferred)

Olive oil

Salt

Pepper

Red potatoes

Mixed vegetables

METHOD

Spray wooden plank and salmon
with olive oil. Sprinkle both sides
of salmon with salt and pepper.
Place salmon fillet on thinner side
of cedar plank. Place salmon in
550° wood fired oven and cook
7–10 minutes, or until completely
done depending on thickness of
fillet. Serve with herb roasted red
potatoes and sautéed fresh
mixed vegetables.

SESAME CHICKEN SALAD

Serves 1-2

INGREDIENTS

Sesame Chicken Salad:

6 oz. chicken breast
(flattened slightly)

Water

Salad oil

Salt

Pepper

Fresh garlic

8-10 wonton skins
cut into 1/8 to 1/4 inch strips

2 tbsp. olive oil

1/2 tsp. sesame seeds

1 tbsp. toasted almonds

Sweet and Sour Dressing:

1 cup sugar

2+ tsp. dry mustard

3/4 cup red wine vinegar

1/8 cup soy vinegar

2 cloves garlic, minced

2 tsp. fresh ginger, minced

2 tsp. lemon juice

1/2 tsp. salt

1/2 tsp. pepper

1 tbsp. sesame oil

2 tbsp. salad oil

METHOD

Preparation requires a
two-day process.

Day 1: Marinate chicken breast
overnight in mixture of your
choice of white wine, water,
salad oil, salt, pepper, and garlic.

Prepare sweet and sour dressing
one day ahead. Add 1 cup sugar,
dry mustard, red wine vinegar,
soy sauce, garlic, ginger, lemon
juice, salt and pepper. Cook on the
top of a boiler for 45 minutes until
it slightly thickens. Add sesame
oil and salad oil. Chill overnight.
Stack 8-10 wonton skins, cut into
1/8 to 1/4 inch strips. Drop into
one inch of hot oil and stir until
strips are crisp and golden brown.
Drain on absorbent paper.

Day 2: Cook chicken on a broiler
or barbecue. While chicken is
cooking, place 8-9 oz. of your
favorite salad mix in a large bowl.
Add 1/2 tsp. sesame seeds and
1 tbsp. toasted almonds. Add 2+
tbsp. sweet and sour dressing
and toss lightly. Place salad in a
serving bowl and top with sliced
chicken breasts. Sprinkle with
fried wontons and a dash more
of sesame seeds.

DOOGER'S SEAFOOD & GRILL

ALTHOUGH BEST KNOWN for ITS CRITICALLY ACCLAIMED CLAM CHOWDER, DOOGER'S FEATURES MANY OTHER AWARD WINNING SEAFOOD DISHES SERVED SAUTÉED, GRILLED, FRIED and CAJUN STYLE.

DOOGER'S SEAFOOD & Grill is located on the south end of town, just before you can see Haystack Rock from Hemlock St. It is within walking distance of many major hotels, and sits about 1/2 mile from the Cannon Beach town center. Although best known for it's critically acclaimed clam chowder, Dooger's features many other award winning seafood dishes served sautéed, grilled, fried and Cajun style. Guests can also enjoy a wide variety of classic fare, including juicy steaks, fettuccini, sandwiches, burgers, salads, and desserts.

Bring your family for a sit down dinner in the dining room, or jump upstairs and have a drink by the fire, in the restaurant's spacious full-service lounge. The atmosphere is homey and pleasant, with a unique touch of beach style. Due to their focus on service and food quality, Dooger's has become a favorite destination for visitors and locals alike.

DOOGER'S CLAM CHOWDER

Serves 6

INGREDIENTS

51 oz. can chopped sea clams

5 oz. Idahoan diced potatoes

1 tbsp. clam base

1/2 tsp. season all

1/4 tsp. white pepper

1/8 tsp. ground thyme

1 quart half & half

1 cup whipping cream

METHOD

Mix all the contents (excluding half & half and whipping cream) together, and let them chill overnight. Add 1 quart half & half and 1 cup whipping cream to the chilled mixture. Bring to a boil on the stove top, stirring frequently. Reduce to a simmer and serve.

STEAK AND LOBSTER

Serves 1

INGREDIENTS

1 hand cut rib-eye steak

Favorite marinade

1 fresh lobster tail

Bay leaves

Cloves

3 strips bacon

METHOD

The steak and lobster dish is a simple, yet tasty favorite at Dooger's. Begin by marinating rib-eye steak with your favorite steak sauce. Grill at 350° for desired length of time depending upon how well done you want your steak. Season lobster with bay leaves and cloves. Steam for 7–9 minutes. Meanwhile, cook bacon in regular oven. Serve steak wrapped in bacon alongside lobster tail.

THE DRIFTWOOD INN

ESTABLISHED IN 1944 AND FORMERLY A SERVICE GARAGE, IT HAS BECOME A UNIQUE PIECE OF CANNON BEACH HISTORY.

THE DRIFTWOOD INN in downtown Cannon Beach has been locally owned and managed for over 60 years. Established in 1944 and formerly a service garage, it has become a unique piece of Cannon Beach history. The walls and shelves inside the restaurant and bar/lounge are adorned with an interesting and eclectic collection of cigarette packages and miniature liquor bottles from years past. The collection was bought by a previous owner from a WWII transfer pilot, who had acquired the items from troops around the world.

The Driftwood prides itself on serving only the highest quality local seafood, steaks and sandwiches. All seafood dishes are prepared with the freshest seafood from the Pacific Ocean, received daily. Samples include Dungeness Crab, Steamer Clams, Bay Shrimp, Halibut, Salmon, Prawns, Razor Clams, and Willapa Bay Oysters.

All of the Driftwood Inn's famous steaks are cut to order, meaning they are not cut until you actually place your order. They will gladly meet your individual needs.

STEAK

Serves 1

All Driftwood steaks are tender beyond compare and downright delicious. Each is cut specifically to your order and broiled to your specifications.

INGREDIENTS

Fresh fillet mignon, New York, or rib-eye cut to your specifications

Salt

Pepper

Garlic butter

METHOD

Add salt, pepper, and garlic butter to your favorite, choice cut of meat. Broil at 350° F for a length of time dependant upon how you want your steak.

DUNGENESS CRAB LOUIE

Serves 1–2

INGREDIENTS

Mixed greens, caesar salad mix, or 1 large head lettuce

2–3 oz. fresh Dungeness Crab meat

2 tomatoes, sliced

2 hardboiled eggs, sliced

2 pickles, sliced

1 oz. olives, sliced

2 lemon wedges

METHOD

On a large plate, lay down your choice of caesar, mixed green, or head lettuce salad. Next, apply a generous portion of Dungeness Crab meat to the greens, followed by sliced tomato, egg, pickle, and olives. Top it off with 3 lemon slices. Apply your favorite dressing, or simply enjoy as is.

ECOLA SEAFOOD

OWNER JAY BECKMAN'S COMMERCIAL FISHING EFFORTS PROVIDE MUCH of THE SALMON, HALIBUT, and OTHER BOTTOM FISH FOR SALE IN THE RESTAURANT.

JAY AND CINDY BECKMAN purchased Ecola Seafood Restaurant and Market in 1993. Located at the corner of 2nd and Spruce across from the city park, Ecola Seafood prides itself on the freshness of its fare. It's truly a family owned and operated restaurant. Owner Jay Beckman's commercial fishing efforts provide much of the salmon, halibut, and other bottom fish for sale in the restaurant. Owner Cindy Beckman's brother provides fresh halibut and commercial crab, while other family members sell their catch to the seafood market and restaurant.

The restaurant features many varieties of fish and chips, homemade clam chowder, crab cakes, seafood cocktails and shellfish available daily. You can also purchase an array of fresh and smoked seafood as well as Ecola Seafood's own brand of canned salmon and tuna. They pride themselves on featuring "Oregon Wild" troll caught salmon.

COCONUT ENCRUSTED TIGER PRAWNS *with* PACIFIC RIM RUM SAUCE

Serves 2–3

INGREDIENTS

20 tiger prawns, peeled and deveined

1 cup flour

1 cup corn starch

4 large eggs, whipped

12 oz. sweetened coconut milk

14 oz. bag of shredded coconut

1 pint Malibu Rum

1/2 cup sugar

Oil

METHOD

Tiger Prawns: Roll prawns in flour, followed by cornstarch. Dip each prawn in whipped egg and roll in 1/2 of shredded coconut. Deep fry until golden brown and done.

Pacific Rum Sauce: In double broiler bring coconut milk, rum, sugar and 7 oz. shredded coconut to a boil. Cook until desired consistency.

HALIBUT STUFFED with DUNGENESS CRAB and CREAMY CRAB SAUCE

Serves 2–3

INGREDIENTS

Halibut:

4 seven oz. fillets of halibut

1 fresh dill sprig

2 medium lemons

1/4 cup lemon juice

4 tbsp. butter

Rind of 2 lemons

Pepper

Olive Oil

8 oz. fresh Dungeness Crab

Creamy Crab Sauce:

1 cup Dungeness Crab meat

1 cup heavy cream

1 cup freshly grated parmesan cheese

Pinch of fresh dill

Salt

Pepper

Chopped green onion for garnish

METHOD

Creamy Crab Sauce: Combine crab meat and cream. Simmer, stirring occasionally. Reduce by half. Add dill, salt and pepper to taste. Fold in cheese and serve immediately.

Halibut Stuffed with Crab: Rinse halibut fillets and pat dry. Slice a pocket of approximately in the center of the fillet and stuff each fillet with 2 oz. of crabmeat. Coat halibut with olive oil and pepper and season lightly with fresh dill.

Place on strip of tin foil. Slice lemon and place one lemon round on top of each halibut fillet. Squeeze remaining juice onto each fillet. Sprinkle lemon rind onto each fillet. Add one tbsp. butter to the top of each fillet Seal foil around halibut.

Bake at 350° for 18 minutes. Check for doneness. Top with dungeness crab sauce and serve hot.

TROPICAL OREGON WILD, TROLL-CAUGHT CHINOOK SALMON with CARAMELIZED MANGO SALSA

Serves 3–4

INGREDIENTS

Salmon:

10 oz. Oregon wild salmon fillet with the skin on

1 cup brown sugar

Salt

Pepper

2 medium lemons, sliced

1 large orange, sliced

1 medium sweet onion, sliced

1/2 cup freshly squeezed orange juice

1 bunch fresh dill, chopped fine

Mango Salsa:

1 large ripe mango, peeled, cored and pureed

1/2 cup freshly squeezed orange juice

2 tbsp. olive oil

1 red bell pepper, diced small

1 small orange flavored vodka

1/2 cup heavy cream

METHOD

Mango Sauce: Place mango in food processor along with 1/2 cup orange juice. Bring to a paste. On high heat in a sauté pan add olive oil and sauté red bell peppers. Add orange flavored vodka to pan. Simmer for 10 minutes.

In a double broiler, add cream and mango paste. Stirring constantly, reduce by half. Add vodka/peppers to mix and continue to cook until desired consistency.

Salmon: Place salmon fillets in foil and rub down with brown sugar, salt and pepper. Place one orange slice on the face of the salmon, followed by a slice of lemon and 1 slice of sweet onion. Mix orange juice, green onion, and dill. Pour over the top of the salmon. Seal foil. Bake at 350° for 20 minutes. After 20 minutes check salmon for doneness. When done serve with mango sauce on top, garnished with dill sprigs.

FULTANO'S PIZZA

HOT OVEN BAKED SUBS ARE MADE IN THEIR TRADITIONAL DECK STYLE PIZZA OVEN. FRESH GARDEN SALADS AND A THIRTY ITEM SALAD BAR PERFECTLY COMPLEMENT your ITALIAN MEAL.

FULTANO'S AT CANNON BEACH opened in the spring of 1994 where the old Whaler Restaurant used to sit. The restaurant is owned and operated by David and Stephanie Johnson, with a little help from their 2-year-old son Matthew! Fultano's specializes in pizza, with over 40 choices of toppings including traditional and gourmet meats and vegetables. You can also choose between five sauce options made in house, and six different cheese varieties.

Although pizza is their specialty, Fultano's is a full Italian eatery with a variety of other menu options. Hot oven-baked subs are made in their traditional deck style pizza oven. Fresh garden salads and a thirty item salad bar perfectly complement your Italian meal. Two pasta selections are available, with your choice of either meat or marinara sauce made in house. Fultano's meat and cheese lasagna is another local favorite, and to top it off, you can sample a variety of desserts and appetizers. Choose from a selection of tap beers, or enjoy a glass of wine before, during, or after your meal.

HOMEMADE ITALIAN MEAT SAUCE

Serves 2

INGREDIENTS

1 lb. quality ground beef

1 lb. sweet Italian sausage

1 small onion finely chopped

1 small green pepper finely chopped

2 ribs celery, diced

2 tbsp. fresh flat leaf
Italian parsley, chopped

1—28 oz. can tomato sauce

1—28 oz. can plum tomatoes
with juice

1/2 tsp. crushed red pepper flakes

1 tbsp. granulated garlic

1 tbsp. dried sweet basil

1 bay leaf

Salt and pepper to taste

METHOD

Coat the bottom of a large, heavy saucepan with olive oil. Brown Italian sausage in olive oil, and cook all the way through. Add vegetables to sausage, and cook over medium heat until veggies start to soften (8–10 minutes). Mix in seasonings and add ground beef. Cook until red in meat is gone. Add both the tomatoes and tomato sauce. Add bay leaf and on medium-low heat simmer 20–30 minutes. Salt and pepper to taste.

Mix sauce with your favorite pasta, preferably cooked al dente. Top with fresh grated Parmesan or a sharper cheese of your choice such as ground Romano. A fresh tossed salad and soft Italian bread would complement the meal nicely.

RICARDO'S PIZZA

Serves 4-6
Chef's Note: Quantity of ingredients will vary according to pizza size and preference

INGREDIENTS

Tomato pizza sauce

Cheese blend: 8 parts mozzarella, 1 part cheddar, and 1 part provolone

Spicy pepperoni, sliced

Julienne cut sun dried tomatoes in olive oil

Black olives, sliced

Prosciutto, sliced

Fresh garlic, chopped

Fresh Chevre (goat cheese)

METHOD

Pizza skin can be purchased pre-made at gourmet or specialty stores. If preferred, use your favorite pizza dough recipe. Cover chosen crust or skin with pizza sauce. Top with cheese, and then cover cheese with sliced pepperoni. Next apply sun-dried tomatoes to pepperoni. Cover with desired quantity of black olive slices. Place prosciutto on top of olives. Sprinkle garlic over olives and top with chevre cheese. Bake according to dough or crust direction and until cheese is melted.

JP'S RESTAURANT

CHEF BILL PAPPAS PROVIDES A VARIETY *of* TANTALIZING CHOICES
FOR LUNCH, DINNER *and* DESSERT, *and* IS RENOWNED
FOR HIS FABULOUS SOUPS.

LOCATED IN THE CENTER of downtown Cannon Beach, JP's restaurant is truly one of Cannon Beach's best. The restaurant was opened in March 1994 by Bill and Diana Pappas, and continues to be a predominantly family-run operation.

Featuring only the freshest local and greater Oregon ingredients, Chef Bill Pappas provides a variety of tantalizing choices for lunch, dinner and dessert, and is renowned for his fabulous soups. The chef can be viewed hard at work through an "Exhibition Kitchen" and food is prepared "Ala Minute", or "Prepared at the minute".

JP's has received numerous distinctions including: "Top 10 food and wine in the Pacific Northwest," and an outstanding rating by "The Mouth of the Columbia." They have also been positively mentioned in the National Geographic Traveler and deemed one of the northwest's best places to eat. The New York Times listed them as a "Can't Miss."

Of course, the most important distinctions come from a loyal clientele, who faithfully return to this special restaurant year after year.

CHICKEN CORDON BLUE

Serves 1

INGREDIENTS

8 oz. chicken breast, butterfly

2 oz. black forest ham, thinly sliced

1 oz. emmental cheese, battinette

3 oz. heavy cream, to coat chicken

2 oz. panko breading, to coat chicken

2 oz. oil, to grill

3 oz. Madeira

1 lemon wedge, to top chicken

METHOD

Begin by butterflying the chicken breast and layer with black forest ham. Place batinette of cheese in the fold in the middle of the breast and close. Place chicken into heavy cream and coat thoroughly. Remove chicken from the cream and place into the breading and cover completely.

Ladle oil onto a hot grill or pan, and place coated chicken breast into hot oil and cook to a golden brown on both sides. When chicken is cooked through, remove it from the heat, making sure to keep it warm. Ladle Madeira sauce onto plate, and then place chicken onto sauce and top with a lemon wedge.

SUGAR-FREE CHEESECAKE

Serves 10

INGREDIENTS

32 oz. cream cheese

8 oz. sour cream

4 eggs

1 cup Splenda artificial sweetener

1/3 cup almonds

1/3 cup macadamia nuts

METHOD

Grind nuts and spread evenly in 10 inch springform pan. Bake at 350° for 15 minutes. Mix cream cheese and sour cream blend unti it is smooth. Next, add sweetener and eggs. Whip until it becomes fluffy and pour over the crust. Bake at 300° for 50 minutes.

JP'S BLACK FOREST SALAD

Serves 1

INGREDIENTS

2 oz. lamb cut in 2 x 1/2 inch laces

2 oz. chicken breast cut in 2 x 1/2 inch laces

1 oz. red onion, julienned

1 oz. mushroom, sliced

1/2 oz. sun-dried tomatoes, julienned

1/2 oz. black olives, sliced

1/2 oz. pine nuts

3 oz. dry red wine (Merlot)

1 oz. balsamic vinegar

1/2 oz. garlic cloves, sliced

2 oz. olive oil

1 oz. mescaline salad mix

METHOD

To a hot sauté pan, add olive oil and heat to a simmer. Add garlic and cook until it starts to brown. Now add the following: lamb, chicken, onions, mushrooms, tomatoes, olives, and pine nuts. Toss and cook in the sauté pan until meat begins to color. Deglaze with wine and vinegar, then cook and toss until the mixture is reduced by two thirds. Place salad mix onto a serving plate and top with sautéed mixture. Serve hot.

MANGO CAFE

THE MENU IS EXTENSIVE and DISHES RANGE FROM OMELETS
FOR BREAKFAST, TO SANDWICHES FOR LUNCH, TO RACK OF
ROASTED LAMB for DINNER

CAFÉ MANGO IS LOCATED ON the north end of Cannon Beach in the Ecola Mall. Enjoy breakfast, lunch or dinner featuring light, healthy cuisine in a casual, friendly atmosphere with just a touch of beach town elegance. Each dish is made with fresh ingredients and prepared to order with a unique Café Mango twist. Café Mango makes an effort to use as many organic foods as possible.

The menu is extensive and dishes range from omelets for breakfast, to sandwiches for lunch, to roasted rack of lamb for dinner. Highlight your meal with a favorite wine, and finish the experience with a sumptuous specialty dessert.

TILAPIA *with* RUM PERFUMED MANGO CREAM SAUCE *and* COUS-COUS SALAD

Serves 1–2

INGREDIENTS

Mango Cream Sauce:

2 1/2 oz. Gold Rum

1 cup mango nectar

3/4 cup heavy cream

Salt and pepper to taste

Tilapia and Cous-Cous Salad:

5–7 oz. tilapia fillets

1 1/2 cups cous-cous

1/2 cup roma tomatoes, diced

2 tsp. fresh basil, chopped

1/3 cup extra virgin olive oil

1/4 cup parmesan cheese, shredded

1/4 cup almonds, toasted and sliced

2 tsp. lemon juice

All-purpose flour, as needed

Salt and pepper to taste

METHOD

Mango Cream Sauce: Heat saucepan on high. Add rum. Use long match or fireplace lighter to ignite rum and burn off alcohol. When the blue flame has died, add mango nectar and reduce by half. Add cream and reduce until thick. Season with salt and pepper and spoon over fish.

Tilapia: Heat a skillet and add 2 tbsp. olive oil. Salt and pepper the tilapia fillets and dredge lightly in flour. Add to hot pan, presentation side down. Cook 2–3 minutes and turn when golden, crispy crust.

Cous-Cous Salad: Cover cous-cous with 2 cups of boiling water in a stainless steel bowl. Cover immediately with plastic wrap. This will steam the cous cous to perfection. Steam for about five minutes then cool slightly.Toss in the tomatoes, basil, olive oil, Parmesan, lemon juice, almonds, and some salt and pepper.

BRICK SEARED BREAST of MUSCOVY DUCK
with DRIED CHERRY BALSAMIC SAUCE

BRICK SEARED BREAST of MUSCOVY DUCK with DRIED CHERRY BALSAMIC SAUCE

Serves 4

INGREDIENTS

Muscovy Duck:

4 Muscovy Duck breasts, boneless

Salt and pepper to taste

1 tbsp. olive oil

Dried Cherry Balsamic Sauce:

3 oz. dried pitted bing cherries

1 pint balsamic vinegar

1/2 cup demi-glace

4 oz. butter, cold

METHOD

Dried Cherry Balsamic Sauce: Reduce vinegar to 1/3 cup, add cherries and demi-glace, bring to a boil. Remove from heat and swirl in cold butter.

Muscovy Duck: Trim breasts of excess fat, pat dry. Carve 1/4 inch deep grid into fat. Season with salt and pepper. Heat Sauté pan and add olive oil. When oil is hot, add duck breasts fat side down. Place foil covered brick on duck for one minute. Turn breasts and cook another 2–3 minutes until medium rare. Do not overcook.

Cut in half on the bias and plate. Spoon on balsamic sauce and serve with wild rice and seasonal vegetables.

Serves 1-2

INGREDIENTS

2 large eggs

1 cup milk

1/3 cup water

1 cup all purpose flour, preferably bleached

1/4 tsp. salt

2 tbsp. butter, melted

1 tbsp. extra virgin olive oil

3 shallots or green onions, (white part only) finely chopped

1 garlic clove, minced

1/2 cup (4 oz.) sliced cultivated white mushrooms

1 Roma tomato, diced

2 tbsp. minced fresh flat leaf parsley

2 eggs

METHOD

This dish is prepared in two separate steps. First create the buckwheat crêpes, then prepare the dish. Blend specific buckwheat crepe ingredients until smooth, approximately 5 seconds. Cover and refrigerate for at least one hour. If the batter has separated, stir gently. Heat crepe pan. Coat the pan lightly with butter (not listed in ingredients), and cook crepe until light golden brown, flip and repeat.

Keep warm or reheat. In large skillet over medium heat, heat the oil and sauté the shallots or green onions and garlic for 1-2 minutes. Add the mushrooms and sauté for 1-2 minutes, or until soft. Stir in the tomatoes and parsley.

Poach the eggs in barely simmering water just until the whites are set and the yolks are still runny. Drain.

Spoon one filling into center of crepe, and top with two eggs. Season with salt and pepper. Fold over three sides of the crepe to form a triangle shape. Garnish plate with black crushed peppers.
Serve immediately.

MO'S RESTAURANT

AND *of* COURSE, NO DINING EXPERIENCE SHOULD BE UNDERTAKEN WITHOUT A TASTE *of* MO'S WORLD-FAMOUS CLAM CHOWDER.

A TRIP TO CANNON BEACH would not be complete without a stop at Mo's. The Mo's franchise has restaurants in various locations on the Oregon Coast. The first was constructed in Newport in 1946 and bore the name "Freddie and Mo's". They came to Cannon Beach some time later, and now sit above the Pacific Ocean south of Haystack Rock.

Mo's features an array of fresh Northwest seafood, and an atmosphere with a distinct coastal-beach flavor. And of course, no dining experience should be undertaken without a taste of Mo's world-famous clam chowder. The Mo's franchise currently produces 500,000 pounds of clam chowder a year; shipped to its restaurants and various grocery stores.

The restaurants have been and continue to be written up in dozens of newspapers around the United States. In 1999 Mo's clam chowder was a featured entrée at the first luncheon ever held in the Smithsonian, which celebrated "Best American Regional Foods." Mo's has truly become an Oregon Coast icon.

MO'S SOURDOUGH BREAD BOWL
CLAM CHOWDER

Serves 4

INGREDIENTS

Red potatoes, diced

Chopped clams

Clam nectar

1 cup onion, chopped

3 slices bacon, diced

*Secret spices

Milk

Flour

1 sourdough bread bowl

METHOD

Begin by cooking bacon until crisp. Dice potatoes, onions, and bacon. Sauté onions in heavy saucepan until softened. Add potatoes and clam nectar; cover and simmer for approximately 15 minutes, or until potatoes are tender.

Remove from heat and add chopped clams, bacon and secret spices. Add milk and flour. Cook over medium heat until clam chowder thickens and bubbles. Stir constantly.

*To order Mo's pre-made secret spices, visit them online www.moschowder.com Just add milk and heat.

FRESH BLACKENED PACIFIC SALMON

Serves 1

INGREDIENTS

Salmon:

8 oz. fillet of your choice of Pacific salmon

Assortment of Cajun spices

Rice pilaf:

Chicken base broth

Long grain Orzo rice

Salt, onion, garlic powder

Turmeric

METHOD

Blackened Salmon: Season 8 oz. salmon fillet with Cajun spices. Grill at 350° for approximately 30 minutes, or until done to your liking. Be sure to grill salmon until blackened to perfection.

Rice Pilaf: Par-boil long grain Orzo rice. Bring chicken base broth to a boil. Add long grain rice to boiling chicken broth, followed by salt, onion, garlic powder, and turmeric. Cover and reduce to low heat until done.

SHRIMP LOUIE *and* MO'S GARLIC CHEESE BREAD

Serves 1–2

INGREDIENTS

Mixed greens

Oregon Bay Shrimp

Carrots, diced

Celery, diced

Black olives, sliced

Tomatoes, sliced

1 hard boiled egg, sliced

Choice of salad dressing

Butter

Garlic powder

Salt

Parmesan cheese

METHOD

Shrimp Louie: Place mixed greens on a plate topped with a healthy serving of Oregon Bay Shrimp. Garnish with diced carrots, celery, black olives, sliced tomatoes and hard-boiled egg. Cover in your choice of salad dressing.

Garlic Cheese Bread: Mix melted margarine or butter with garlic powder, salt and parmesan cheese. Spread on sourdough bread and cook until done.

PIZZA A' FETTA

THEY SERVE HAND-TOSSED GOURMET PIZZAS, HOUSE SALADS, HOMEMADE PASTA, MINESTRONE SOUP, OREGON and ITALIAN MICRO-BREWED BEER, WINE, and SOFT DRINKS.

PIZZA A' FETTA WAS purchased by the current owners with two goals in mind: creating a destination restaurant and achieving recognition as an iconic Cannon Beach restaurant. By concentrating on 3 crucial elements: product quality, service, and atmosphere, these goals have been achieved.

By combining family culinary methods of preparation, special recipes, and the finest quality ingredients available, Pizza a' Fetta has become one of the top 100 Pizzerias in the U.S. as voted by Pizza Today Magazine!

At Pizza a' Fetta, you will find a welcoming, friendly staff and a pleasant traditional atmosphere. They serve hand-tossed gourmet pizzas, house salads, homemade pasta, minestrone soup, Oregon and Italian micro-brewed beer and wines, and soft drinks. All sauces and dressings are made in-house, and they cordially invite you to come enjoy an authentic Old World pizza. Pizza a' Fetta always serves up their most famous special; unequaled taste.

MONTRACHET PIZZA

Serves 2–4

INGREDIENTS

Pizza:

16 oz. doughball

3 oz. olive oil (Infused with garlic and sun-dried tomatoes)

12 oz. mozzarella cheese

1 1/2 oz. sun-dried tomatoes, dried

4 oz. fresh mushrooms, sliced

4 oz. fresh Roma tomato, sliced

1 oz. Montrachet Goat Cheese, soft

Basil

Oregano

1/2 oz. parmesan cheese

Dough:

2 tsp. active dry yeast

1 tsp. sugar

1/2 tsp. salt

1 tbsp. olive oil

1/2 cup warm water

1 1/2 cups all-purpose (plain) flour

Infused Olive Oil:

8 oz. garlic cloves

8 oz. sun-dried tomatoes

16 fl/oz. extra virgin olive oil

METHOD

Dough: Combine yeast, sugar, salt, olive oil, and water in a bowl. Mix and set aside for around 10 minutes, or until frothy. In another bowl, place the flour and make a well in the center. Add the yeast mixture in the well. Combine by gradually incorporating the flour into the yeast mixture (by hand), adding a little extra water if necessary. Transfer the dough to a floured board and knead until it is smooth and elastic, about 5 minutes. Place the dough in a large, lightly oiled bowl. Cover and place in a warm, draft-free place for 30 minutes or until doubled in size. Makes one 14 inch pizza base. Preparation time 50 minutes.

Infused Olive Oil: Combine garlic and sun-dried tomatoes in a food processor, mix for one minute. Add olive oil and mix for another minute. Makes 32 fl/oz. infused olive oil. Preparation time 5 minutes.

Pizza: Pre-heat electric oven to 475˚ (525˚ for gas). Flour pizza pan. Stretch dough ball to 14 inches in diameter. Lay a thin layer of infused olive oil on the stretched dough. Evenly distribute sun-dried tomatoes, mozzarella cheese, Roma tomatoes, mushrooms, Montrachet cheese, basil, oregano, and parmesan cheese. Bake approximately 10–12 minutes on center rack of oven. Be sure to keep a constant watch on pizza. It should brown at 7 minutes, and be removed at 8–12 minutes. The pizza is ready when the cheese is bubbling and the crust is brown on the top and bottom.

STEPHANIE INN

EXECUTIVE CHEF JOHN NEWMAN OVERSEES the TASTEFUL ORCHESTRATION of TASTE, FLAVOR, COLOR AND TEXTURE THAT TAKES PLACE EACH DAY WITHIN the KITCHEN.

OVERLOOKING THE Pacific Ocean on the south end of Cannon Beach, the Stephanie Inn provides patrons with a world-class dining experience. Executive Chef John Newman, who has overseen the Stephanie Inn's kitchen operations since March 1998, oversees a tasteful orchestration of taste, flavor, color and texture that takes place each day within the kitchen.

Calling on the region's top growers, fishermen, foragers and winemakers, the kitchen relies on an abundance of fresh local ingredients to fashion their masterpieces.

Making sauces, grilling vegetables, preparing garnishes, grilling meats and seafood and making salads for up to 80 people all takes place in the confines of a tiny kitchen, where everyone works comfortably side by side. Nightly menus feature only the freshest, best quality foods the region has to offer, served in very innovative ways.

One of Cannon Beach's finest; a dining experience at the Stephanie Inn is not to be missed!

AHI & PRAWN DISH

Serves 1–2

INGREDIENTS

5 1/2 oz. Ahi Tuna

2 each prawns

Juice of 1 red pepper

2 each snow peas

1 each lemon ring

1 garlic top

Pea tendrils

1 oz. Orzo Pasta

1 slice of fennel

METHOD

Juice red pepper and reduce in saucepan until thickened. Season and sear the Ahi Tuna to medium rare. Season & saute prawns, then season and sauté snow peas. Cut lemon ring out of lemon; cook in 2 oz. sugar and 2 oz. water until tender-approximately 8 minutes. Cook Orzo Pasta, then slice and season fennel, roasted in oven until tender, approximately 8–10 minutes.

STEPHANIE INN SCONES

Makes 12 scones

INGREDIENTS

2 1/2 cups all-purpose flour

1/2 cup sugar

1 tbsp. baking powder

1/2 tbsp. salt

1 cup chopped fresh or dried fruit, nuts, chocolate chips or a combination of flavors

1 1/4 cups heavy cream

METHOD

Depending on the season, these scones might be flavored with chopped nuts, dried fruits such as dried apricots, dried cherries, raisins, fresh mango, or blackberries. The best way to maintain tenderness in the scones is to work the dough as little as possible after adding the cream—only until it binds together and can be rolled out on a lightly floured surface. Preheat the oven to 350° F.

In a large mixing bowl, whisk or stir the dry ingredients together, mixing thoroughly. Stir in the fruit or nuts, and then slowly stir in the cream, just until the mixture comes together. Turn the dough onto a lightly floured surface and gently pat the mixture into a round or square shape. Sprinkle with flour and roll to approximately 1/2 inch thickness. Cut into rounds, triangles, or squares. Place on a greased baking sheet and brush with additional heavy cream. Sprinkle with sugar and bake for about 15–20 minutes or until lightly golden.

NEW YORK STRIPLOIN STEAK
PARSLEY OIL & VEAL STOCK REDUCTION

Serves 6–8

INGREDIENTS

6 pounds whole New York striploin steak, trimmed of fat and sinew

Salt and freshly ground black pepper to taste

1/4 cup canola oil

METHOD

To begin, the chef recommends calling your butcher or grocer ahead to order this cut of meat. The Stephanie Inn chefs often serve this dish with a veal-stock reduction sauce (demi-glace) and parsley oil drizzled on the side. A favorite barbecue sauce would also work well.

Preheat the oven to 375° F.

Season the beef liberally with kosher salt and white pepper. Heat the canola oil in a large, heavy-bottomed skillet over medium-high heat. Add the meat to the hot oil and sear it for about 2 minutes on each side, or until golden brown. Place the seared beef on a baking sheet in the preheated oven and roast for about 10 to 15 minutes or until a meat thermometer registers 125° F (medium rare) or is done to your desired specifications.

To serve: Allow the beef to sit at room temperature for at least 5 minutes and then slice into 3/4 inch thick slices. Place the beef slices on pre-warmed plates. Drizzle approximately 2 tbsp. warm veal reduction sauce around each serving of beef, and then drizzle each plate with 1 tbsp. parsley oil.

HUCKLEBERRY CHEESECAKE
and HUCKLEBERRY SAUCE

Serves 12–16

INGREDIENTS

Graham Cracker Crust:

2 cups graham cracker crumbs

1/2 cup sugar

1/2 cup (1 stick) unsalted butter, melted

Cream Cheese Huckleberry Filling:

2 1/2 cups cream cheese, softened

1 cup sugar

1 tbsp. vanilla extract

6 eggs, room temperature

1 cup huckleberries or blueberries

Huckleberry Sauce:

1 1/2 cups huckleberries

1/2 cup water

1 cup sugar

2 tbsp. cornstarch mixed with 2 tbl water

METHOD

The chef prefers wild blue huckleberries from the Oregon Coast, but blueberries will work well as a substitute. This cheesecake needs to chill at least 4 hours before serving. Chilling overnight is recommended.

Graham Cracker Crust: Preheat the oven to 325° F. In a mixing bowl, combine the graham cracker crumbs and sugar. Stir in the melted butter, mixing well. Grease the bottom of a 10 inch spring-form pan. Pour the crust mixture into the pan and use the back of a soupspoon to press it evenly over the bottom of the pan and 1 inch up the sides. Chill the crust until it is firm.

Cream Cheese Huckleberry Filling: In a mixing bowl, beat the softened cream cheese at high speed until it is smooth and creamy. Reduce the speed and add the sugar, mixing well. Add the eggs, one at a time, scraping down the sides of the bowl as necessary, then add the vanilla. Beat until the ingredients in the mixture are well incorporated. Fold 1 cup of huckleberries into the mixture, and them pour it into the prepared crust. Bake the cheesecake in the preheated oven for about 1 hour and 15 minutes, or until a knife inserted in the center comes out almost clean. Remove the cheesecake from the oven and cool on a wire rack until it is cool enough to handle. Chill the cheesecake at least 4 hours before serving.

Huckleberry Sauce: Combine the huckleberries, sugar, and water in a saucepan over medium-high heat. Bring the mixture to a boil, and then reduce the heat to a simmer and cook, stirring often for about 15 minutes. In a small bowl, mix the cornstarch with 2 tbsp. water. Stir the cornstarch into the huckleberries, stirring constantly until slightly thickened.

To serve: Run a knife around the edges of the spring-form pan to loosen the crust. Remove cheesecake from the pan and slice into 12–16 portions. Serve cheesecake on dessert plates and ladle a large spoonful of huckleberry sauce over the top of each serving.

PIG'N PANCAKE

KNOWN FOR the QUALITY OF ITS BREAKFAST MEALS, the PIG'N PANCAKE TAKES SPECIAL PRIDE IN ITS MANY UNIQUE SPECIALTY PANCAKES.

THE ORIGINAL PIG N' Pancake restaurant was opened in May 1961 in Seaside with $100 and $2000 worth of borrowed equipment. The newest Cannon Beach location was opened in 1997, on the south end of downtown Cannon Beach off Hemlock St. The uniquely constructed dining area is elevated and overlooks the bustling downtown, giving the effect of dining in a large "tree house".

Known for the quality of its breakfast meals, the Pig'n Pancake takes special pride in its many unique specialty pancakes. The recipes for Buttermilk, Swedish, Sourdough and French Batter pancakes are original recipes that have been used from the very beginning. The Pig'n Pancake in Cannon Beach currently serves breakfast, lunch and dinner. The restaurant provides a wonderful dining experience for all types of patrons, and the family friendly atmosphere is especially noteworthy.

WESTERN OMELET

Serves 1

INGREDIENTS

1/4 of a large onion, diced

1/4 of a medium green pepper, diced

1/4 of a medium tomato, diced

2–3 oz. cheddar cheese, diced into

1/4 inch cubes

3 eggs

METHOD

Dice onion and green pepper and mix together. Dice cheddar cheese in to 1/4 inch cubes, followed by tomato. Whip 3 eggs and place into an oiled pan. Add 1 tbsp. diced onion and green peppers, followed by 1 tbsp. each tomato and cheese. When mixture is dry around the edges, fold over in half. Cook to your liking.

To finish, place desired amount of cheese on top of omelet, followed by tomato as a garnish. Recommended serving with pancakes or potatoes.

BABY BACK RIBS

Serves 1

INGREDIENTS

1 qt. + 16 oz. of your favorite barbecue sauce

5 choice ribs

Salt

Pepper

METHOD

Salt and pepper the 5 ribs and place in an oven to brown at 350° for 30 minutes. After browning ribs, take 16 oz. of barbecue sauce and equal part water. In a large bowl mix barbecue sauce and water. Place ribs in a large pan and cover completely with barbecue sauce mixture. Foil cook at 350° for approximately 3 1/2 hours. Make sure you do not over cook to the point of the meat falling from the bones. Take the remaining barbecue sauce mixture and heat to cover ribs when serving.

WAYFARER RESTAURANT & LOUNGE

WHEN DINING, ENJOY A LOVELY VIEW of THE PACIFIC OCEAN FROM THE DINING ROOM, or RELAX IN WARMER WEATHER UNDER AN UMBRELLA ON the OUTSIDE DECK.

THE WAYFARER Restaurant and Lounge has long been a favorite Cannon Beach dining destination. Located just south of the town center, the menu highlights the very best fare our region has to offer. Choose a time of day that suites you; the menu offers choices for breakfast, lunch and dinner. When dining, enjoy a lovely view of the Pacific Ocean from the dining room, or relax in warmer weather under an umbrella on the outside deck.

They take pride in the overall cleanliness of the atmosphere, décor and cuisine presentation. The extensive menu features only the freshest seafood available presented in an intriguing variety of textures and flavors. Accompany your meal with a selection from the extensive wine, beer, or cocktail lists. The wine list features a wide selection of Northwest and California choices.

Most noticeable is the quality and attention to service. Restaurant guests will enjoy interacting with a staff that is attentive, sincere, and caring; a true reflection of what is most important at The Wayfarer. You will indeed come away with a sense of freshness and satisfaction.

SEARED SALMON *with* CUCUMBER-CAPER BERRY RELISH

Serves 6

INGREDIENTS

Salmon:

6–seven oz. wild salmon fillet portions

Salt

Fresh ground pepper

Pomade olive oil

Cucumber-Caper Berry Relish:

6 cucumbers, peel, seed, dice

4 roma tomatoes, diced

1/2 bu. scallions, diced

1/2 bu. dill, chopped

1 cup caper berries, sliced

1/4 cup sugar

1/2 cup champagne vinegar

Salt and fresh ground pepper

Combine all

METHOD

Begin by seasoning salmon fillet portions. In a large sauté pan heat oil and sear the seasoned salmon to a golden brown on the top side. Finish salmon in the oven and top with relish.

CHICKEN-CHEDDAR APPLE SALAD

Serves 6

INGREDIENTS

Chicken Mix:

2 lb. fresh spinach, cleaned and picked

3 tart apples, cored and diced

1 lb. Tillamook smoked cheddar, diced

1/2 lb. toasted sliced almonds

3 large boneless, skinless chicken breast—cooked, chilled, and diced

Dressing:

1 cup mayonnaise

1/2 tsp. granulated garlic

1 dash tabasco sauce

2 tbsp. sugar

2 tbsp. white vinegar

Salt and pepper

METHOD

Cook chicken breast, chill, and dice. Mix diced tart apples, 1 lb. Tillamook smoked cheddar, toasted sliced almonds, and diced boneless chicken breast, chill. Divide spinach on plates, top with chicken mix, garnish with cherry tomatoes or grilled bread, and add 1 cup dressing.

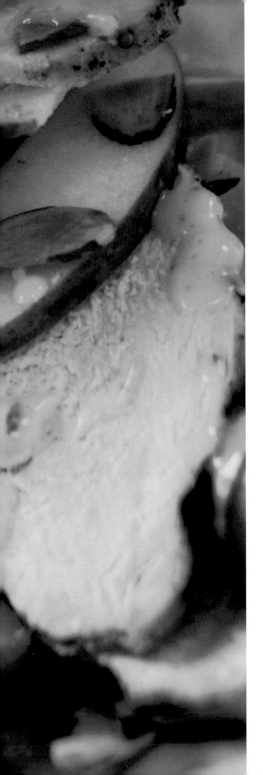

Bon Appêtit

A DARK, ILLIMITABLE OCEAN
without bound, without dimension,
where length, breadth, and height, and time and
place are lost. *John Milton - "Paradise Lost"*

ACKNOWLEDGEMENTS

We would like to begin by offering a special thank you to all those who supported us and believed in this project as fiercely as we did. Kat Nyberg; for your art, joy, and inspiration. You helped us make this happen. Our parents: Don and Barb, Jeff and Jean; the Masterson and Carlsen families –THANK YOU! James Faurentino; you believed in us from the beginning. Mark Piscitelli; you listened to everything. Thanks for your literary excellence, support, and friendship. Melisa Kroening; for your honesty and support! Tina McBride; you have helped create something brilliant. Very special thank you to Ursula K. LeGuin, Terry Brooks, and Peter Lindsey for your contributions. Thank you to all the Cannon Beach restaurants that participated in this project. You were all so helpful in making this a reality.

We would also like to thank: Elizabeth Morrow-McKenzie, Jim (Jimmy G) Graceffo – you were always so supportive, Kim, Sharon, and Charlene at the Chamber of Commerce, Jay and Laura Stewart, Sharon Stewart and The Cannon Beach Historical Society, Boomer and Lisa Reiff, The Nyberg family, The Cannon Beach Conference Center, Bruce's Candy Kitchen, Cannon Beach Cookie Company, John Williams, Tom and Cat Mauldin and The Cannon Beach Gazette, Osburn's, U.S. Bank, Mariner Market, The Landing, Bill's Tavern, Tom Drumheller, Tom and Lori Jiroudek at The Bald Eagle, Kim Barnett and The Bronze Coast Gallery, Rhodes-Stringfellow Gallery, The Dragonfire Gallery, Cannon Beach Surf, Sandpiper Square, Duane Johnson, Uncle Jay, David Robinson, Mike Stanley and Mike's Bike Shop, Marlene Laws, Kris Betts, Bob and Gladie Kaleta, Cory and Brook Burnett, The Little People, Don Howell & Surf Crest Market, Jeff Womack, Roger Wendlick, The Smithsonian Institution, Yale Collection of Western Americana, Beinecke Rare Book and Manuscript Library.

CREDITS

PHOTOGRAPHERS : Anderson, Don : pp. 66, 67. Bonn, Rick : pp 69. Burnett, Cory : pp 118. Dennison, Hal : pp 55. Hernandez, Rodolfo: cover photo. Kroening, Melisa : pp. 42, 119, 122. Masterson, Donald Scott : pp. 5, 8, 14, 33, 34, 37, 38, 44, 45, 48, 52, 53, 54, 56, 61, 62, 68, 78, 79, 81, 87, 94, 95, 96, 97, 106, 109, 111, 113, 115, 119, 122. www.donaldscott3.com. Nyberg, Kat : pp: 5, 32, 40, 44, 61, 62, 71, 79, 103, 123, 124. www.katnybergphotography.com. Robinson, Thomas : pp. 5, 51, 54, 57, 69, 121, dust jacket. Studarus, David : pp. 5, 76, 117, dust jacket. Vetter, George : pp. 5, 35, 38, 39, 44, 58, 59, 64, 67, 69, 70, 121, dust jacket, www.cannon-beach.net. Bob Welsh : pp. 49. ARTISTS : Flores, Oscar : pp. 36. Gorsuch, Richard: pp. 41. Hull, Jeffery : pp. 9, 30, 31, dust jacket. Peterson, Peter : pp. 60. Schmidt, Geoff : pp. 47, 50. Steidel, Bill : pp. 7, 120. Tieman, Michael : pp. 43. HISTORICAL : The Alvena Nyberg Private Collection : 5, 13, 15, 16, 17, 19, 20, 24. Cannon Beach Historical Society : pp. 5, 15, 16, 17, 18, 19, 23, 26, 43, 64, fold out. Jeff Womack : pp. 5, 16, 19, 28. The Smithsonian Institution : pp. 10 & 11. Yale Collection of Western Americana, Beinecke Rare Book and Manuscript Library : Atlas Map # 93 published 1983- pp. 12. The Cannon Beach Conference Center : pp. 16, 17, 26, 27, 29, 46. Don Howell & Surf Crest Market : pp. 19. Cannon Beach Cookie Company : 27. Anderson Sundry Co. : pp. 5, 28. Smith-Western Inc. : pp. 28. Cannon Beach Gazette : pp. 65. SOURCES : Lindsey, Peter, Comin' in Over the Rock : A Storyteller's History of Cannon Beach. Cannon Beach : Saddle Mountain Press, 2004. O'Donnell, Terence, Cannon Beach: A Place by the Sea. Portland : Oregon Historical Society Press, 1996. GENERAL : Collections of the Cannon Beach Historical Society; Steidel, Bill; Laws, Marlene; Betts, Kris; Williams, John Lindsey, Peter; Goodenough, Heather; Seaside Signal; The Cannon Beach Gazette, Jay Stewart Pottery, Cannon Beach Chamber of Commerce : pp. 5, sandcastle poster fold out.